# 50 Ice Cream Flavors You Haven't Tried Yet

By: Kelly Johnson

# Table of Contents

- Avocado Lime Ice Cream
- Earl Grey and Lavender Ice Cream
- Black Sesame Ice Cream
- Blueberry Basil Ice Cream
- Olive Oil and Sea Salt Ice Cream
- Pineapple Jalapeño Ice Cream
- Matcha White Chocolate Ice Cream
- Ginger Peach Ice Cream
- Turmeric Honey Ice Cream
- Lemon Poppy Seed Ice Cream
- Sweet Corn and Raspberry Swirl Ice Cream
- Strawberry Balsamic Ice Cream
- Coconut Lemongrass Ice Cream
- Rosemary Fig Ice Cream
- Mascarpone and Blackberry Ice Cream
- Ube (Purple Yam) Ice Cream
- Black Garlic Ice Cream
- Cherry Cola Ice Cream
- Mango Chili Ice Cream
- Saffron Pistachio Ice Cream
- Cucumber Mint Ice Cream
- Chai Spiced Ice Cream
- Peanut Butter Curry Ice Cream
- Watermelon and Feta Ice Cream
- Chocolate Wasabi Ice Cream
- Carrot Cake Ice Cream
- Bourbon Pecan Ice Cream
- Yuzu Sorbet Ice Cream
- Blue Cheese and Pear Ice Cream
- Salted Licorice Ice Cream
- Pumpkin Spice Latte Ice Cream
- Chocolate and Chili Ice Cream
- Grapefruit Campari Ice Cream
- White Chocolate Lavender Ice Cream
- Almond Butter and Jelly Ice Cream

- Maple Bacon Ice Cream
- Mocha Chipotle Ice Cream
- Honeycomb Crunch Ice Cream
- Sweet Potato Marshmallow Ice Cream
- Hibiscus Sorbet Ice Cream
- Mango Lassi Ice Cream
- Cereal Milk Ice Cream
- Lychee Rose Ice Cream
- Lemon Curd Ice Cream
- Espresso Cardamom Ice Cream
- Tahini Chocolate Chip Ice Cream
- Pine Nut and Honey Ice Cream
- Matcha and Red Bean Ice Cream
- Brown Butter Sage Ice Cream
- Beet and Goat Cheese Ice Cream

## Avocado Lime Ice Cream

**Ingredients**

- 2 ripe avocados
- 1 cup heavy cream
- 1/2 cup whole milk
- 3/4 cup granulated sugar (or honey for a natural option)
- 1/4 cup fresh lime juice (about 2–3 limes)
- 1 tablespoon lime zest
- Pinch of salt
- Optional: 1/2 teaspoon vanilla extract

**Instructions**

1. **Prepare the avocados**:
    - Slice the avocados in half, remove the pit, and scoop out the flesh into a blender or food processor.
2. **Blend the mixture**:
    - Add heavy cream, milk, sugar, lime juice, lime zest, salt, and vanilla extract (if using) to the blender with the avocado. Blend until smooth and creamy.
3. **Chill the mixture**:
    - Transfer the mixture to a bowl, cover, and refrigerate for at least 2 hours to allow the flavors to meld and the mixture to chill thoroughly.
4. **Churn the ice cream**:
    - Pour the chilled mixture into an ice cream maker and churn according to the manufacturer's instructions (usually 20–30 minutes).
5. **Freeze**:
    - Transfer the churned ice cream to an airtight container and freeze for at least 4 hours or until firm.
6. **Serve**:
    - Scoop into bowls or cones, garnish with extra lime zest, and enjoy!

# Earl Grey and Lavender Ice Cream

## Ingredients

- 2 cups heavy cream
- 1 cup whole milk
- 3/4 cup granulated sugar
- 3 Earl Grey tea bags
- 1 tablespoon dried lavender
- 4 large egg yolks
- Pinch of salt

## Instructions

1. **Steep the flavors**: Heat the milk, cream, and sugar in a saucepan over medium heat until warm (but not boiling). Add the tea bags and lavender, then steep for 15–20 minutes. Remove tea bags and strain out the lavender.
2. **Make the custard**: In a bowl, whisk egg yolks. Slowly pour the warm cream mixture into the yolks while whisking, then return the mixture to the saucepan. Cook over low heat, stirring constantly, until it thickens slightly (about 170°F/77°C).
3. **Chill and churn**: Strain the custard, chill it in the refrigerator for at least 2 hours, then churn in an ice cream maker.
4. **Freeze**: Transfer to an airtight container and freeze until firm.

**Black Sesame Ice Cream**

**Ingredients**

- 1/4 cup black sesame seeds
- 2 cups heavy cream
- 1 cup whole milk
- 3/4 cup sugar
- 4 large egg yolks
- Pinch of salt

**Instructions**

1. **Toast the sesame seeds**: Heat the sesame seeds in a dry pan over medium heat until fragrant, about 2–3 minutes. Grind the seeds into a paste using a food processor or mortar and pestle.
2. **Prepare the custard**: In a saucepan, heat the milk, sugar, and sesame paste until warm. In a separate bowl, whisk the egg yolks. Slowly pour the warm mixture into the yolks, whisking constantly, then return to the saucepan. Cook over low heat, stirring until it thickens.
3. **Chill and churn**: Strain the custard, chill it, then churn in an ice cream maker.
4. **Freeze**: Transfer to a container and freeze until ready to serve.

# Blueberry Basil Ice Cream

## Ingredients

- 1 cup fresh blueberries
- 2 tablespoons sugar
- 2 cups heavy cream
- 1 cup whole milk
- 3/4 cup sugar
- 1/4 cup fresh basil leaves
- 4 large egg yolks
- 1 tablespoon lemon juice

## Instructions

1. **Cook the blueberries**: In a small saucepan, cook blueberries with 2 tablespoons of sugar over medium heat until they burst and form a thick sauce. Set aside to cool.
2. **Infuse the basil**: Heat the milk, cream, and sugar with basil leaves in a saucepan over medium heat. Let the basil steep for 10–15 minutes, then strain.
3. **Make the custard**: Whisk egg yolks in a bowl, then slowly add the warm basil-infused cream. Cook over low heat until thickened.
4. **Combine and churn**: Stir in the blueberry sauce and lemon juice, chill the mixture, and churn in an ice cream maker.
5. **Freeze**: Transfer to an airtight container and freeze until firm.

## Olive Oil and Sea Salt Ice Cream

### Ingredients:

- 2 cups (500 ml) heavy cream
- 1 cup (250 ml) whole milk
- 1/2 cup (100 g) granulated sugar
- 4 large egg yolks
- 1/3 cup (80 ml) high-quality extra virgin olive oil
- 1/4 tsp flaky sea salt (like Maldon or fleur de sel), plus more for garnish
- 1 tsp vanilla extract

### Instructions:

1. **Heat the Base**
   - In a medium saucepan, combine the heavy cream, milk, and half of the sugar. Heat over medium heat until the edges start to simmer (do not boil).
2. **Prepare the Egg Mixture**
   - In a separate bowl, whisk the egg yolks with the remaining sugar until pale and slightly thickened.
3. **Temper the Eggs**
   - Slowly pour a ladle of the hot cream mixture into the egg yolk mixture, whisking constantly to avoid scrambling the eggs.
   - Gradually add the tempered egg mixture back into the saucepan with the remaining cream.
4. **Cook the Custard**
   - Stir the mixture over medium-low heat, continuously stirring until it thickens enough to coat the back of a spoon (about 170-175°F / 77-80°C). Do not let it boil.
5. **Cool the Base**
   - Strain the custard through a fine-mesh sieve into a bowl to remove any curdled bits. Stir in the vanilla extract and olive oil until smooth.
   - Cover the bowl and chill in the refrigerator for at least 4 hours or overnight.
6. **Churn the Ice Cream**
   - Once the base is thoroughly chilled, pour it into your ice cream maker and churn according to the manufacturer's instructions.
7. **Add Sea Salt & Freeze**

- After churning, transfer the ice cream to a container. Sprinkle in 1/4 tsp of sea salt and gently swirl it through the ice cream. Cover and freeze for 3-4 hours, or until firm.
8. **Serve and Garnish**
    - Scoop the ice cream into bowls or cones. Drizzle with a bit more olive oil and sprinkle a pinch of flaky sea salt on top for extra flavor.

Enjoy this creamy, aromatic treat with an elegant balance of sweetness and savory saltiness!

# Ginger Peach Ice Cream

## Ingredients:

- 2 cups ripe peaches, peeled and diced
- 1 cup (250 ml) heavy cream
- 1 cup (250 ml) whole milk
- 3/4 cup (150 g) granulated sugar
- 1-2 tbsp freshly grated ginger (adjust to taste)
- 1 tsp vanilla extract
- 1 tbsp lemon juice

## Instructions:

1. **Prepare Peach Mixture**
   - In a blender, puree the diced peaches until smooth. Strain the puree through a fine mesh sieve to remove any pulp if desired.
2. **Combine Ingredients**
   - In a medium saucepan, combine the heavy cream, whole milk, sugar, grated ginger, and lemon juice. Heat over medium heat until warm but not boiling.
3. **Add Peach Puree**
   - Remove from heat and stir in the peach puree and vanilla extract.
4. **Cool the Mixture**
   - Allow the mixture to cool to room temperature, then cover and chill in the refrigerator for at least 4 hours or overnight.
5. **Churn the Ice Cream**
   - Once chilled, pour the mixture into an ice cream maker and churn according to the manufacturer's instructions.
6. **Freeze and Serve**
   - Transfer the ice cream to a container and freeze for 3-4 hours until firm. Serve scoops with additional diced peaches or a sprinkle of ginger for garnish.

# Pineapple Jalapeño Ice Cream

## Ingredients:

- 2 cups fresh pineapple, chopped
- 1 cup (250 ml) heavy cream
- 1 cup (250 ml) whole milk
- 3/4 cup (150 g) granulated sugar
- 1/2 cup (120 ml) fresh lime juice
- 1-2 jalapeños, finely chopped (seeds removed for less heat)
- 1 tsp vanilla extract

## Instructions:

1. **Prepare Pineapple Mixture**
   - In a blender, puree the fresh pineapple until smooth. Strain the puree through a fine mesh sieve to remove the pulp if desired.
2. **Combine Ingredients**
   - In a medium saucepan, combine the heavy cream, whole milk, sugar, lime juice, and chopped jalapeños. Heat over medium heat until the mixture is warm but not boiling.
3. **Add Pineapple Puree**
   - Remove the saucepan from heat and stir in the pineapple puree and vanilla extract.
4. **Cool the Mixture**
   - Allow the mixture to cool to room temperature, then cover and chill in the refrigerator for at least 4 hours or overnight.
5. **Churn the Ice Cream**
   - Once chilled, pour the mixture into an ice cream maker and churn according to the manufacturer's instructions.
6. **Freeze and Serve**
   - Transfer the ice cream to a container and freeze for 3-4 hours until firm. Scoop and serve, garnished with extra pineapple or jalapeño slices if desired.

# Matcha White Chocolate Ice Cream

## Ingredients:

- 2 cups (500 ml) heavy cream
- 1 cup (250 ml) whole milk
- 3/4 cup (150 g) granulated sugar
- 4 large egg yolks
- 1/2 cup white chocolate chips
- 2 tbsp matcha green tea powder
- 1 tsp vanilla extract

## Instructions:

1. **Heat the Base**
   - In a medium saucepan, heat the heavy cream, whole milk, and half of the sugar over medium heat until it begins to simmer.
2. **Prepare the Egg Mixture**
   - In a bowl, whisk together the egg yolks and the remaining sugar until thick and pale.
3. **Temper the Eggs**
   - Gradually add a small amount of the hot cream mixture to the egg yolks, whisking constantly. Then pour the egg mixture back into the saucepan.
4. **Cook the Custard**
   - Cook over medium-low heat, stirring until the mixture thickens and coats the back of a spoon (about 170-175°F / 77-80°C). Remove from heat.
5. **Melt the Chocolate and Matcha**
   - In a separate bowl, combine the white chocolate chips and matcha powder. Pour the hot custard over the mixture and stir until the chocolate melts and everything is smooth. Stir in the vanilla extract.
6. **Cool and Churn**
   - Allow the mixture to cool to room temperature, then refrigerate for at least 4 hours or overnight. Churn in an ice cream maker according to the manufacturer's instructions.
7. **Freeze and Serve**
   - Transfer the ice cream to a container and freeze for 3-4 hours until firm. Serve scoops garnished with extra matcha powder or white chocolate shavings.

**Ginger Peach Ice Cream**

**Ingredients:**

- 2 cups ripe peaches, peeled and diced
- 1 cup (250 ml) heavy cream
- 1 cup (250 ml) whole milk
- 3/4 cup (150 g) granulated sugar
- 1-2 tbsp freshly grated ginger (adjust to taste)
- 1 tsp vanilla extract
- 1 tbsp lemon juice

**Instructions:**

1. **Prepare Peach Mixture**
   - In a blender, puree the diced peaches until smooth. Strain the puree through a fine mesh sieve to remove any pulp if desired.
2. **Combine Ingredients**
   - In a medium saucepan, combine the heavy cream, whole milk, sugar, grated ginger, and lemon juice. Heat over medium heat until warm but not boiling.
3. **Add Peach Puree**
   - Remove from heat and stir in the peach puree and vanilla extract.
4. **Cool the Mixture**
   - Allow the mixture to cool to room temperature, then cover and chill in the refrigerator for at least 4 hours or overnight.
5. **Churn the Ice Cream**
   - Once chilled, pour the mixture into an ice cream maker and churn according to the manufacturer's instructions.
6. **Freeze and Serve**
   - Transfer the ice cream to a container and freeze for 3-4 hours until firm. Serve scoops with additional diced peaches or a sprinkle of ginger for garnish.

**Turmeric Honey Ice Cream**

**Ingredients:**

- 1 cup (250 ml) heavy cream
- 1 cup (250 ml) whole milk
- 3/4 cup (150 g) granulated sugar
- 1/2 cup honey
- 1 tsp turmeric powder
- 1/2 tsp vanilla extract
- Pinch of salt

**Instructions:**

1. **Combine Ingredients**
    - In a medium saucepan, whisk together the heavy cream, whole milk, sugar, honey, turmeric powder, vanilla extract, and salt.
2. **Heat the Mixture**
    - Heat over medium heat until the mixture is warm but not boiling, stirring frequently.
3. **Cool the Mixture**
    - Remove from heat and let it cool to room temperature. Cover and refrigerate for at least 4 hours or overnight.
4. **Churn the Ice Cream**
    - Once chilled, pour the mixture into an ice cream maker and churn according to the manufacturer's instructions.
5. **Freeze and Serve**
    - Transfer the ice cream to a container and freeze for 3-4 hours until firm. Serve and enjoy!

# Lemon Poppy Seed Ice Cream

## Ingredients:

- 2 cups (500 ml) heavy cream
- 1 cup (250 ml) whole milk
- 3/4 cup (150 g) granulated sugar
- Zest of 2 lemons
- 1/2 cup fresh lemon juice
- 1/4 cup poppy seeds
- 1 tsp vanilla extract

## Instructions:

1. **Combine Ingredients**
   - In a medium bowl, whisk together the heavy cream, whole milk, sugar, lemon zest, lemon juice, poppy seeds, and vanilla extract.
2. **Cool the Mixture**
   - Refrigerate the mixture for at least 2 hours until well chilled.
3. **Churn the Ice Cream**
   - Pour the chilled mixture into an ice cream maker and churn according to the manufacturer's instructions.
4. **Freeze and Serve**
   - Transfer the ice cream to a container and freeze for 3-4 hours until firm. Scoop and serve with extra lemon zest on top if desired.

# Sweet Corn and Raspberry Swirl Ice Cream

## Ingredients:

- 2 cups fresh corn kernels (from about 4 ears of corn)
- 1 cup (250 ml) heavy cream
- 1 cup (250 ml) whole milk
- 3/4 cup (150 g) granulated sugar
- 1/2 tsp vanilla extract
- 1 cup fresh raspberries
- 2 tbsp lemon juice

## Instructions:

1. **Prepare Corn Base**
   - In a saucepan, combine the corn kernels, heavy cream, whole milk, and sugar. Heat over medium heat until warm.
2. **Blend the Mixture**
   - Blend the mixture until smooth, then strain through a fine mesh sieve to remove the solids. Stir in the vanilla extract.
3. **Cool the Base**
   - Allow the mixture to cool to room temperature, then cover and chill in the refrigerator for at least 4 hours or overnight.
4. **Prepare Raspberry Swirl**
   - In a small saucepan, combine raspberries and lemon juice. Cook over medium heat until the raspberries break down and form a sauce. Strain to remove seeds and set aside to cool.
5. **Churn the Ice Cream**
   - Pour the chilled corn mixture into an ice cream maker and churn according to the manufacturer's instructions.
6. **Swirl and Freeze**
   - Once churned, gently fold in the raspberry sauce. Transfer to a container and freeze for 3-4 hours until firm. Scoop and enjoy!

# Strawberry Balsamic Ice Cream

## Ingredients:

- 2 cups fresh strawberries, hulled and sliced
- 1 cup (250 ml) heavy cream
- 1 cup (250 ml) whole milk
- 3/4 cup (150 g) granulated sugar
- 2 tbsp balsamic vinegar
- 1 tsp vanilla extract

## Instructions:

1. **Prepare Strawberry Mixture**
   - In a bowl, combine the sliced strawberries with 1/4 cup of sugar and balsamic vinegar. Let sit for 30 minutes to macerate.
2. **Blend the Mixture**
   - In a blender, puree the macerated strawberries until smooth.
3. **Combine Ingredients**
   - In a separate bowl, whisk together the heavy cream, whole milk, remaining sugar, and vanilla extract.
4. **Add Strawberry Puree**
   - Stir in the strawberry puree until well combined.
5. **Chill and Churn**
   - Refrigerate the mixture for at least 2 hours until chilled. Pour into an ice cream maker and churn according to the manufacturer's instructions.
6. **Freeze and Serve**
   - Transfer the ice cream to a container and freeze for 3-4 hours until firm. Serve with fresh strawberries and a drizzle of balsamic vinegar if desired.

# Coconut Lemongrass Ice Cream

## Ingredients:

- 2 cups coconut milk
- 1 cup (250 ml) heavy cream
- 3/4 cup (150 g) granulated sugar
- 1-2 stalks lemongrass, chopped
- 1 tsp vanilla extract

## Instructions:

1. **Infuse the Coconut Milk**
   - In a saucepan, combine coconut milk, heavy cream, sugar, and lemongrass. Heat over medium heat until warm.
2. **Steep the Mixture**
   - Remove from heat and let the mixture steep for about 30 minutes. Strain out the lemongrass pieces.
3. **Cool and Churn**
   - Stir in the vanilla extract, then cool the mixture to room temperature. Refrigerate for at least 4 hours or overnight.
4. **Churn the Ice Cream**
   - Pour the chilled mixture into an ice cream maker and churn according to the manufacturer's instructions.
5. **Freeze and Serve**
   - Transfer to a container and freeze for 3-4 hours until firm. Serve with toasted coconut on top if desired.

**Rosemary Fig Ice Cream**

**Ingredients:**

- 2 cups fresh figs, chopped
- 1 cup (250 ml) heavy cream
- 1 cup (250 ml) whole milk
- 3/4 cup (150 g) granulated sugar
- 2-3 sprigs fresh rosemary
- 1 tsp vanilla extract

**Instructions:**

1. **Infuse the Cream**
    - In a saucepan, heat the heavy cream, milk, sugar, and rosemary over medium heat until warm.
2. **Cool and Steep**
    - Remove from heat and let steep for 30 minutes. Strain out the rosemary.
3. **Combine Ingredients**
    - Stir in the figs and vanilla extract.
4. **Chill and Churn**
    - Refrigerate the mixture for at least 4 hours or overnight. Pour into an ice cream maker and churn according to the manufacturer's instructions.
5. **Freeze and Serve**
    - Transfer to a container and freeze for 3-4 hours until firm. Serve garnished with extra figs or rosemary.

# Mascarpone and Blackberry Ice Cream

## Ingredients:

- 1 cup (250 g) mascarpone cheese
- 1 cup (250 ml) heavy cream
- 1 cup (250 ml) whole milk
- 3/4 cup (150 g) granulated sugar
- 1 cup fresh blackberries
- 1 tsp vanilla extract

## Instructions:

1. **Prepare Blackberry Sauce**
    - In a saucepan, heat blackberries and 1/4 cup of sugar over medium heat until the blackberries break down. Strain out seeds and set aside to cool.
2. **Combine Ice Cream Base**
    - In a bowl, whisk together mascarpone cheese, heavy cream, whole milk, remaining sugar, and vanilla extract until smooth.
3. **Chill the Mixture**
    - Refrigerate the mixture for at least 2 hours until chilled.
4. **Churn the Ice Cream**
    - Pour the chilled mixture into an ice cream maker and churn according to the manufacturer's instructions.
5. **Swirl and Freeze**
    - Once churned, gently fold in the blackberry sauce. Transfer to a container and freeze for 3-4 hours until firm. Serve with fresh blackberries on top if desired.

**Ube (Purple Yam) Ice Cream**

**Ingredients:**

- 1 cup ube puree (canned or homemade)
- 1 cup (250 ml) heavy cream
- 1 cup (250 ml) whole milk
- 3/4 cup (150 g) granulated sugar
- 1 tsp vanilla extract

**Instructions:**

1. **Combine Ingredients**
   - In a medium bowl, whisk together the ube puree, heavy cream, whole milk, sugar, and vanilla extract until well blended.
2. **Chill the Mixture**
   - Refrigerate the mixture for at least 2 hours until chilled.
3. **Churn the Ice Cream**
   - Pour the chilled mixture into an ice cream maker and churn according to the manufacturer's instructions.
4. **Freeze and Serve**
   - Transfer to a container and freeze for 3-4 hours until firm. Scoop and enjoy the vibrant color and flavor!

**Black Garlic Ice Cream**

**Ingredients:**

- 1 cup (250 ml) heavy cream
- 1 cup (250 ml) whole milk
- 3/4 cup (150 g) granulated sugar
- 4-5 cloves black garlic, mashed
- 1 tsp vanilla extract
- Pinch of salt

**Instructions:**

1. **Combine Ingredients**
    - In a saucepan, whisk together the heavy cream, whole milk, sugar, black garlic, vanilla extract, and salt.
2. **Heat the Mixture**
    - Heat over medium heat until warm, stirring frequently to dissolve the sugar.
3. **Cool the Mixture**
    - Remove from heat and let it cool to room temperature. Cover and refrigerate for at least 4 hours or overnight.
4. **Churn the Ice Cream**
    - Once chilled, pour the mixture into an ice cream maker and churn according to the manufacturer's instructions.
5. **Freeze and Serve**
    - Transfer the ice cream to a container and freeze for 3-4 hours until firm. Scoop and enjoy the unique flavor!

**Cherry Cola Ice Cream**

**Ingredients:**

- 1 cup (250 ml) heavy cream
- 1 cup (250 ml) whole milk
- 3/4 cup (150 g) granulated sugar
- 1 cup cherry cola (or any cola)
- 1/2 cup fresh cherries, pitted and chopped
- 1 tsp vanilla extract

**Instructions:**

1. **Combine Ingredients**
    - In a medium bowl, whisk together the heavy cream, whole milk, sugar, cherry cola, and vanilla extract until the sugar is dissolved.
2. **Chill the Mixture**
    - Refrigerate for at least 2 hours until well chilled.
3. **Churn the Ice Cream**
    - Pour the chilled mixture into an ice cream maker and churn according to the manufacturer's instructions.
4. **Add Cherries**
    - Once churned, gently fold in the chopped cherries.
5. **Freeze and Serve**
    - Transfer to a container and freeze for 3-4 hours until firm. Serve and enjoy the fizzy, fruity delight!

**Mango Chili Ice Cream**

**Ingredients:**

- 2 cups ripe mango puree
- 1 cup (250 ml) heavy cream
- 1 cup (250 ml) whole milk
- 3/4 cup (150 g) granulated sugar
- 1-2 tsp chili powder (adjust to taste)
- 1 tsp lime juice

**Instructions:**

1. **Combine Ingredients**
    - In a bowl, whisk together the mango puree, heavy cream, whole milk, sugar, chili powder, and lime juice until smooth.
2. **Chill the Mixture**
    - Refrigerate for at least 2 hours until chilled.
3. **Churn the Ice Cream**
    - Pour the chilled mixture into an ice cream maker and churn according to the manufacturer's instructions.
4. **Freeze and Serve**
    - Transfer to a container and freeze for 3-4 hours until firm. Serve with a sprinkle of chili powder on top if desired.

# Saffron Pistachio Ice Cream

## Ingredients:

- 1 cup (250 ml) heavy cream
- 1 cup (250 ml) whole milk
- 3/4 cup (150 g) granulated sugar
- 1/4 cup pistachios, finely chopped
- 1/4 tsp saffron threads, soaked in 2 tbsp warm milk
- 1 tsp vanilla extract

## Instructions:

1. **Combine Ingredients**
   - In a saucepan, whisk together the heavy cream, whole milk, sugar, and saffron milk over medium heat until warm.
2. **Add Pistachios**
   - Stir in the chopped pistachios and vanilla extract.
3. **Cool the Mixture**
   - Remove from heat and let it cool to room temperature. Refrigerate for at least 4 hours or overnight.
4. **Churn the Ice Cream**
   - Once chilled, pour the mixture into an ice cream maker and churn according to the manufacturer's instructions.
5. **Freeze and Serve**
   - Transfer to a container and freeze for 3-4 hours until firm. Enjoy the rich flavors of saffron and pistachio!

## Cucumber Mint Ice Cream

### Ingredients:

- 1 cup cucumber puree (from peeled cucumbers)
- 1 cup (250 ml) heavy cream
- 1 cup (250 ml) whole milk
- 3/4 cup (150 g) granulated sugar
- 1/4 cup fresh mint leaves, finely chopped
- 1 tsp lemon juice
- Pinch of salt

### Instructions:

1. **Combine Ingredients**
   - In a bowl, whisk together the cucumber puree, heavy cream, whole milk, sugar, mint, lemon juice, and salt until well mixed.
2. **Chill the Mixture**
   - Refrigerate for at least 2 hours until chilled.
3. **Churn the Ice Cream**
   - Pour the chilled mixture into an ice cream maker and churn according to the manufacturer's instructions.
4. **Freeze and Serve**
   - Transfer to a container and freeze for 3-4 hours until firm. Serve garnished with extra mint leaves if desired.

# Chai Spiced Ice Cream

## Ingredients:

- 2 cups (500 ml) heavy cream
- 1 cup (250 ml) whole milk
- 3/4 cup (150 g) granulated sugar
- 4-5 chai tea bags
- 1 tsp vanilla extract

## Instructions:

1. **Infuse the Cream**
    - In a saucepan, heat the heavy cream, whole milk, and sugar over medium heat until warm.
2. **Add Tea Bags**
    - Remove from heat and steep the chai tea bags for 15 minutes.
3. **Cool and Strain**
    - Remove the tea bags and let the mixture cool to room temperature.
4. **Add Vanilla and Chill**
    - Stir in the vanilla extract, then refrigerate for at least 4 hours or overnight.
5. **Churn the Ice Cream**
    - Pour the chilled mixture into an ice cream maker and churn according to the manufacturer's instructions.
6. **Freeze and Serve**
    - Transfer to a container and freeze for 3-4 hours until firm. Enjoy the warm spices in a cool treat!

**Peanut Butter Curry Ice Cream**

**Ingredients:**

- 1 cup (250 ml) heavy cream
- 1 cup (250 ml) whole milk
- 3/4 cup (150 g) granulated sugar
- 1/2 cup creamy peanut butter
- 1-2 tsp curry powder (adjust to taste)
- 1 tsp vanilla extract

**Instructions:**

1. **Combine Ingredients**
   - In a bowl, whisk together the heavy cream, whole milk, sugar, peanut butter, curry powder, and vanilla extract until smooth.
2. **Chill the Mixture**
   - Refrigerate for at least 2 hours until well chilled.
3. **Churn the Ice Cream**
   - Pour the chilled mixture into an ice cream maker and churn according to the manufacturer's instructions.
4. **Freeze and Serve**
   - Transfer to a container and freeze for 3-4 hours until firm. Enjoy this unique flavor combination!

## Watermelon and Feta Ice Cream

### Ingredients:

- 2 cups watermelon puree (from seedless watermelon)
- 1 cup (250 ml) heavy cream
- 1 cup (250 ml) whole milk
- 3/4 cup (150 g) granulated sugar
- 1/2 cup crumbled feta cheese
- 1 tbsp lemon juice

### Instructions:

1. **Combine Ingredients**
    - In a bowl, whisk together the watermelon puree, heavy cream, whole milk, sugar, and lemon juice until smooth.
2. **Chill the Mixture**
    - Refrigerate for at least 2 hours until well chilled.
3. **Churn the Ice Cream**
    - Pour the chilled mixture into an ice cream maker and churn according to the manufacturer's instructions.
4. **Add Feta**
    - Once churned, gently fold in the crumbled feta cheese.
5. **Freeze and Serve**
    - Transfer to a container and freeze for 3-4 hours until firm. Serve garnished with extra feta if desired.

**Chocolate Wasabi Ice Cream**

**Ingredients:**

- 1 cup (250 ml) heavy cream
- 1 cup (250 ml) whole milk
- 3/4 cup (150 g) granulated sugar
- 1 cup dark chocolate, chopped
- 1-2 tsp wasabi paste (adjust to taste)
- 1 tsp vanilla extract

**Instructions:**

1. **Melt Chocolate**
   In a saucepan, heat the heavy cream and whole milk over medium heat until warm. Remove from heat and add the chopped chocolate, stirring until melted and smooth.
2. **Add Wasabi**
   Stir in the wasabi paste and vanilla extract until well combined.
3. **Cool the Mixture**
   Let the mixture cool to room temperature, then refrigerate for at least 4 hours or overnight.
4. **Churn the Ice Cream**
   Pour the chilled mixture into an ice cream maker and churn according to the manufacturer's instructions.
5. **Freeze and Serve**
   Transfer to a container and freeze for 3-4 hours until firm. Enjoy the unique flavor combination!

**Carrot Cake Ice Cream**

**Ingredients:**

- 2 cups (500 ml) heavy cream
- 1 cup (250 ml) whole milk
- 3/4 cup (150 g) granulated sugar
- 1 cup grated carrots
- 1 tsp cinnamon
- 1/2 tsp nutmeg
- 1/2 cup chopped walnuts or pecans
- 1/2 cup cream cheese, softened

**Instructions:**

1. **Combine Ingredients**
   In a bowl, whisk together the heavy cream, whole milk, sugar, grated carrots, cinnamon, nutmeg, and cream cheese until smooth.
2. **Chill the Mixture**
   Refrigerate for at least 2 hours until well chilled.
3. **Churn the Ice Cream**
   Pour the chilled mixture into an ice cream maker and churn according to the manufacturer's instructions.
4. **Add Nuts**
   Gently fold in the chopped walnuts or pecans.
5. **Freeze and Serve**
   Transfer to a container and freeze for 3-4 hours until firm. Enjoy the delightful taste of carrot cake!

**Bourbon Pecan Ice Cream**

**Ingredients:**

- 1 cup (250 ml) heavy cream
- 1 cup (250 ml) whole milk
- 3/4 cup (150 g) granulated sugar
- 1/2 cup pecans, chopped
- 1/4 cup bourbon
- 1 tsp vanilla extract

**Instructions:**

1. **Combine Ingredients**
   In a saucepan, heat the heavy cream, whole milk, and sugar over medium heat until warm.
2. **Add Bourbon and Pecans**
   Stir in the bourbon, chopped pecans, and vanilla extract.
3. **Cool the Mixture**
   Let the mixture cool to room temperature, then refrigerate for at least 4 hours or overnight.
4. **Churn the Ice Cream**
   Pour the chilled mixture into an ice cream maker and churn according to the manufacturer's instructions.
5. **Freeze and Serve**
   Transfer to a container and freeze for 3-4 hours until firm. Enjoy the nutty and boozy flavor!

## Yuzu Sorbet Ice Cream

### Ingredients:

- 1 cup yuzu juice (fresh or bottled)
- 1 cup (250 ml) water
- 3/4 cup (150 g) granulated sugar
- 1 tsp lemon juice

### Instructions:

1. **Combine Ingredients**
   In a saucepan, combine the yuzu juice, water, sugar, and lemon juice. Heat over medium heat until the sugar dissolves.
2. **Chill the Mixture**
   Remove from heat and let it cool to room temperature. Refrigerate for at least 2 hours.
3. **Churn the Sorbet**
   Pour the chilled mixture into an ice cream maker and churn according to the manufacturer's instructions.
4. **Freeze and Serve**
   Transfer to a container and freeze for 3-4 hours until firm. Enjoy the refreshing citrus flavor!

**Blue Cheese and Pear Ice Cream**

**Ingredients:**

- 1 cup (250 ml) heavy cream
- 1 cup (250 ml) whole milk
- 3/4 cup (150 g) granulated sugar
- 1/2 cup blue cheese, crumbled
- 1 cup ripe pear, pureed
- 1 tsp vanilla extract

**Instructions:**

1. **Combine Ingredients**
   In a saucepan, heat the heavy cream and whole milk over medium heat until warm.
2. **Add Cheese and Pear**
   Stir in the blue cheese, pear puree, and vanilla extract until smooth.
3. **Cool the Mixture**
   Let the mixture cool to room temperature, then refrigerate for at least 4 hours or overnight.
4. **Churn the Ice Cream**
   Pour the chilled mixture into an ice cream maker and churn according to the manufacturer's instructions.
5. **Freeze and Serve**
   Transfer to a container and freeze for 3-4 hours until firm. Enjoy the savory and sweet contrast!

# Salted Licorice Ice Cream

## Ingredients:

- 1 cup (250 ml) heavy cream
- 1 cup (250 ml) whole milk
- 3/4 cup (150 g) granulated sugar
- 1/2 cup salted licorice, chopped
- 1 tsp vanilla extract

## Instructions:

1. **Combine Ingredients**
   In a saucepan, heat the heavy cream and whole milk over medium heat until warm.
2. **Add Licorice**
   Stir in the chopped salted licorice and vanilla extract.
3. **Cool the Mixture**
   Let the mixture cool to room temperature, then refrigerate for at least 4 hours or overnight.
4. **Churn the Ice Cream**
   Pour the chilled mixture into an ice cream maker and churn according to the manufacturer's instructions.
5. **Freeze and Serve**
   Transfer to a container and freeze for 3-4 hours until firm. Enjoy the unique flavor of salty licorice!

## Pumpkin Spice Latte Ice Cream

### Ingredients:

- 2 cups (500 ml) heavy cream
- 1 cup (250 ml) whole milk
- 3/4 cup (150 g) granulated sugar
- 1 cup pumpkin puree
- 2 tsp pumpkin spice mix
- 1/2 cup brewed coffee, cooled

### Instructions:

1. **Combine Ingredients**
   In a bowl, whisk together the heavy cream, whole milk, sugar, pumpkin puree, pumpkin spice mix, and brewed coffee until smooth.
2. **Chill the Mixture**
   Refrigerate for at least 2 hours until well chilled.
3. **Churn the Ice Cream**
   Pour the chilled mixture into an ice cream maker and churn according to the manufacturer's instructions.
4. **Freeze and Serve**
   Transfer to a container and freeze for 3-4 hours until firm. Enjoy this seasonal favorite!

**Chocolate and Chili Ice Cream**

**Ingredients:**

- 1 cup (250 ml) heavy cream
- 1 cup (250 ml) whole milk
- 3/4 cup (150 g) granulated sugar
- 1 cup dark chocolate, chopped
- 1-2 tsp chili powder (adjust to taste)
- 1 tsp vanilla extract

**Instructions:**

1. **Melt Chocolate**
   In a saucepan, heat the heavy cream and whole milk over medium heat until warm. Remove from heat and add the chopped chocolate, stirring until melted and smooth.
2. **Add Chili**
   Stir in the chili powder and vanilla extract until well combined.
3. **Cool the Mixture**
   Let the mixture cool to room temperature, then refrigerate for at least 4 hours or overnight.
4. **Churn the Ice Cream**
   Pour the chilled mixture into an ice cream maker and churn according to the manufacturer's instructions.
5. **Freeze and Serve**
   Transfer to a container and freeze for 3-4 hours until firm. Enjoy the spicy chocolate treat!

# Grapefruit Campari Ice Cream

## Ingredients:

- 1 cup (250 ml) heavy cream
- 1 cup (250 ml) whole milk
- 3/4 cup (150 g) granulated sugar
- 1 cup grapefruit juice (freshly squeezed)
- 1/4 cup Campari
- 1 tsp vanilla extract

## Instructions:

1. **Combine Ingredients**
   In a bowl, whisk together the heavy cream, whole milk, sugar, grapefruit juice, Campari, and vanilla extract until well mixed.
2. **Chill the Mixture**
   Refrigerate for at least 2 hours until well chilled.
3. **Churn the Ice Cream**
   Pour the chilled mixture into an ice cream maker and churn according to the manufacturer's instructions.
4. **Freeze and Serve**
   Transfer to a container and freeze for 3-4 hours until firm. Enjoy the refreshing and slightly bitter flavor!

# White Chocolate Lavender Ice Cream

## Ingredients:

- 1 cup (250 ml) heavy cream
- 1 cup (250 ml) whole milk
- 3/4 cup (150 g) granulated sugar
- 1/2 cup white chocolate, chopped
- 2 tsp dried lavender buds
- 1 tsp vanilla extract

## Instructions:

1. **Heat Cream and Lavender**
   In a saucepan, heat the heavy cream and dried lavender over medium heat until warm. Remove from heat and let steep for 15 minutes.
2. **Melt White Chocolate**
   Strain the lavender from the cream and return the cream to the saucepan. Add the chopped white chocolate and stir until melted and smooth.
3. **Combine Ingredients**
   Whisk in the whole milk, sugar, and vanilla extract until well combined.
4. **Chill the Mixture**
   Let the mixture cool to room temperature, then refrigerate for at least 4 hours or overnight.
5. **Churn the Ice Cream**
   Pour the chilled mixture into an ice cream maker and churn according to the manufacturer's instructions.
6. **Freeze and Serve**
   Transfer to a container and freeze for 3-4 hours until firm. Enjoy the floral and creamy flavor!

## Almond Butter and Jelly Ice Cream

### Ingredients:

- 1 cup (250 ml) heavy cream
- 1 cup (250 ml) whole milk
- 3/4 cup (150 g) granulated sugar
- 1/2 cup almond butter
- 1/2 cup fruit jelly or jam (your choice)
- 1 tsp vanilla extract

### Instructions:

1. **Combine Ingredients**
   In a bowl, whisk together the heavy cream, whole milk, sugar, almond butter, and vanilla extract until smooth.
2. **Chill the Mixture**
   Refrigerate for at least 2 hours until well chilled.
3. **Churn the Ice Cream**
   Pour the chilled mixture into an ice cream maker and churn according to the manufacturer's instructions.
4. **Add Jelly**
   During the last few minutes of churning, add dollops of fruit jelly or jam and gently fold it into the ice cream.
5. **Freeze and Serve**
   Transfer to a container and freeze for 3-4 hours until firm. Enjoy this delicious twist on a classic!

## Maple Bacon Ice Cream

### Ingredients:

- 1 cup (250 ml) heavy cream
- 1 cup (250 ml) whole milk
- 3/4 cup (150 g) granulated sugar
- 1/2 cup maple syrup
- 1/2 cup cooked and crumbled bacon
- 1 tsp vanilla extract

### Instructions:

1. **Combine Ingredients**
   In a bowl, whisk together the heavy cream, whole milk, sugar, maple syrup, and vanilla extract until smooth.
2. **Chill the Mixture**
   Refrigerate for at least 2 hours until well chilled.
3. **Churn the Ice Cream**
   Pour the chilled mixture into an ice cream maker and churn according to the manufacturer's instructions.
4. **Add Bacon**
   During the last few minutes of churning, fold in the crumbled bacon.
5. **Freeze and Serve**
   Transfer to a container and freeze for 3-4 hours until firm. Enjoy the sweet and savory flavor!

## Mocha Chipotle Ice Cream

### Ingredients:

- 1 cup (250 ml) heavy cream
- 1 cup (250 ml) whole milk
- 3/4 cup (150 g) granulated sugar
- 1/2 cup brewed coffee, cooled
- 1-2 tsp chipotle powder (adjust to taste)
- 1 tsp vanilla extract
- 1/2 cup chocolate chips

### Instructions:

1. **Combine Ingredients**
   In a bowl, whisk together the heavy cream, whole milk, sugar, brewed coffee, chipotle powder, and vanilla extract until smooth.
2. **Chill the Mixture**
   Refrigerate for at least 2 hours until well chilled.
3. **Churn the Ice Cream**
   Pour the chilled mixture into an ice cream maker and churn according to the manufacturer's instructions.
4. **Add Chocolate Chips**
   During the last few minutes of churning, add the chocolate chips.
5. **Freeze and Serve**
   Transfer to a container and freeze for 3-4 hours until firm. Enjoy the bold and spicy flavor!

## Honeycomb Crunch Ice Cream

### Ingredients:

- 1 cup (250 ml) heavy cream
- 1 cup (250 ml) whole milk
- 3/4 cup (150 g) granulated sugar
- 1/2 cup honeycomb candy, crushed
- 1 tsp vanilla extract

### Instructions:

1. **Combine Ingredients**
   In a bowl, whisk together the heavy cream, whole milk, sugar, and vanilla extract until smooth.
2. **Chill the Mixture**
   Refrigerate for at least 2 hours until well chilled.
3. **Churn the Ice Cream**
   Pour the chilled mixture into an ice cream maker and churn according to the manufacturer's instructions.
4. **Add Honeycomb**
   During the last few minutes of churning, fold in the crushed honeycomb candy.
5. **Freeze and Serve**
   Transfer to a container and freeze for 3-4 hours until firm. Enjoy the crunchy and sweet flavor!

# Sweet Potato Marshmallow Ice Cream

## Ingredients:

- 1 cup (250 ml) heavy cream
- 1 cup (250 ml) whole milk
- 3/4 cup (150 g) granulated sugar
- 1 cup sweet potato puree
- 1/2 cup marshmallow fluff
- 1 tsp vanilla extract

## Instructions:

1. **Combine Ingredients**
   In a bowl, whisk together the heavy cream, whole milk, sugar, sweet potato puree, marshmallow fluff, and vanilla extract until smooth.
2. **Chill the Mixture**
   Refrigerate for at least 2 hours until well chilled.
3. **Churn the Ice Cream**
   Pour the chilled mixture into an ice cream maker and churn according to the manufacturer's instructions.
4. **Freeze and Serve**
   Transfer to a container and freeze for 3-4 hours until firm. Enjoy the creamy and sweet flavor!

# Hibiscus Sorbet Ice Cream

## Ingredients:

- 1 cup hibiscus tea (brewed and cooled)
- 1 cup (250 ml) water
- 3/4 cup (150 g) granulated sugar
- 1 tbsp lemon juice

## Instructions:

1. **Combine Ingredients**
   In a saucepan, combine the hibiscus tea, water, sugar, and lemon juice. Heat over medium heat until the sugar dissolves.
2. **Chill the Mixture**
   Remove from heat and let it cool to room temperature. Refrigerate for at least 2 hours.
3. **Churn the Sorbet**
   Pour the chilled mixture into an ice cream maker and churn according to the manufacturer's instructions.
4. **Freeze and Serve**
   Transfer to a container and freeze for 3-4 hours until firm. Enjoy the refreshing floral flavor!

**Mango Lassi Ice Cream**

**Ingredients:**

- 1 cup (250 ml) heavy cream
- 1 cup (250 ml) whole milk
- 3/4 cup (150 g) granulated sugar
- 1 cup mango puree (fresh or canned)
- 1/2 cup plain yogurt
- 1 tsp cardamom powder
- 1 tsp vanilla extract

**Instructions:**

1. **Combine Ingredients**
   In a bowl, whisk together the heavy cream, whole milk, sugar, mango puree, yogurt, cardamom powder, and vanilla extract until well mixed.
2. **Chill the Mixture**
   Refrigerate for at least 2 hours until well chilled.
3. **Churn the Ice Cream**
   Pour the chilled mixture into an ice cream maker and churn according to the manufacturer's instructions.
4. **Freeze and Serve**
   Transfer to a container and freeze for 3-4 hours until firm. Enjoy the tropical and creamy flavor!

**Cereal Milk Ice Cream**

**Ingredients:**

- 1 cup (250 ml) heavy cream
- 1 cup (250 ml) whole milk
- 3/4 cup (150 g) granulated sugar
- 1 cup cereal of your choice (e.g., cornflakes)
- 1 tsp vanilla extract

**Instructions:**

1. **Infuse Milk**
   In a bowl, combine the cereal with the whole milk and let it steep for 30 minutes. Strain the mixture to remove the cereal.
2. **Combine Ingredients**
   In a separate bowl, whisk together the heavy cream, sugar, and vanilla extract with the infused milk until well combined.
3. **Chill the Mixture**
   Refrigerate for at least 2 hours until well chilled.
4. **Churn the Ice Cream**
   Pour the chilled mixture into an ice cream maker and churn according to the manufacturer's instructions.
5. **Freeze and Serve**
   Transfer to a container and freeze for 3-4 hours until firm. Enjoy the nostalgic and creamy flavor!

**Lychee Rose Ice Cream**

**Ingredients:**

- 1 cup (250 ml) heavy cream
- 1 cup (250 ml) whole milk
- 3/4 cup (150 g) granulated sugar
- 1 cup lychee puree (fresh or canned)
- 2 tsp rose water
- 1 tsp vanilla extract

**Instructions:**

1. **Combine Ingredients**
   In a bowl, whisk together the heavy cream, whole milk, sugar, lychee puree, rose water, and vanilla extract until smooth.
2. **Chill the Mixture**
   Refrigerate for at least 2 hours until well chilled.
3. **Churn the Ice Cream**
   Pour the chilled mixture into an ice cream maker and churn according to the manufacturer's instructions.
4. **Freeze and Serve**
   Transfer to a container and freeze for 3-4 hours until firm. Enjoy the floral and fruity flavor!

**Lemon Curd Ice Cream**

**Ingredients:**

- 1 cup (250 ml) heavy cream
- 1 cup (250 ml) whole milk
- 3/4 cup (150 g) granulated sugar
- 1/2 cup lemon curd (store-bought or homemade)
- 1 tsp vanilla extract

**Instructions:**

1. **Combine Ingredients**
   In a bowl, whisk together the heavy cream, whole milk, sugar, lemon curd, and vanilla extract until well mixed.
2. **Chill the Mixture**
   Refrigerate for at least 2 hours until well chilled.
3. **Churn the Ice Cream**
   Pour the chilled mixture into an ice cream maker and churn according to the manufacturer's instructions.
4. **Freeze and Serve**
   Transfer to a container and freeze for 3-4 hours until firm. Enjoy the tangy and creamy flavor!

**Espresso Cardamom Ice Cream**

**Ingredients:**

- 1 cup (250 ml) heavy cream
- 1 cup (250 ml) whole milk
- 3/4 cup (150 g) granulated sugar
- 1/2 cup brewed espresso, cooled
- 1 tsp cardamom powder
- 1 tsp vanilla extract

**Instructions:**

1. **Combine Ingredients**
   In a bowl, whisk together the heavy cream, whole milk, sugar, espresso, cardamom powder, and vanilla extract until well combined.
2. **Chill the Mixture**
   Refrigerate for at least 2 hours until well chilled.
3. **Churn the Ice Cream**
   Pour the chilled mixture into an ice cream maker and churn according to the manufacturer's instructions.
4. **Freeze and Serve**
   Transfer to a container and freeze for 3-4 hours until firm. Enjoy the rich and aromatic flavor!

## Tahini Chocolate Chip Ice Cream

**Ingredients:**

- 1 cup (250 ml) heavy cream
- 1 cup (250 ml) whole milk
- 3/4 cup (150 g) granulated sugar
- 1/2 cup tahini
- 1 tsp vanilla extract
- 1/2 cup chocolate chips

**Instructions:**

1. **Combine Ingredients**
   In a bowl, whisk together the heavy cream, whole milk, sugar, tahini, and vanilla extract until smooth.
2. **Chill the Mixture**
   Refrigerate for at least 2 hours until well chilled.
3. **Churn the Ice Cream**
   Pour the chilled mixture into an ice cream maker and churn according to the manufacturer's instructions.
4. **Add Chocolate Chips**
   During the last few minutes of churning, fold in the chocolate chips.
5. **Freeze and Serve**
   Transfer to a container and freeze for 3-4 hours until firm. Enjoy the nutty and sweet flavor!

# Pine Nut and Honey Ice Cream

## Ingredients:

- 1 cup (250 ml) heavy cream
- 1 cup (250 ml) whole milk
- 3/4 cup (150 g) granulated sugar
- 1/2 cup pine nuts, toasted
- 1/4 cup honey
- 1 tsp vanilla extract

## Instructions:

1. **Combine Ingredients**
   In a bowl, whisk together the heavy cream, whole milk, sugar, honey, and vanilla extract until well mixed.
2. **Chill the Mixture**
   Refrigerate for at least 2 hours until well chilled.
3. **Churn the Ice Cream**
   Pour the chilled mixture into an ice cream maker and churn according to the manufacturer's instructions.
4. **Add Pine Nuts**
   During the last few minutes of churning, fold in the toasted pine nuts.
5. **Freeze and Serve**
   Transfer to a container and freeze for 3-4 hours until firm. Enjoy the nutty and sweet flavor!

# Matcha and Red Bean Ice Cream

## Ingredients:

- 1 cup (250 ml) heavy cream
- 1 cup (250 ml) whole milk
- 3/4 cup (150 g) granulated sugar
- 2 tbsp matcha powder
- 1/2 cup sweetened red bean paste
- 1 tsp vanilla extract

## Instructions:

1. **Combine Ingredients**
   In a bowl, whisk together the heavy cream, whole milk, sugar, matcha powder, and vanilla extract until well combined.
2. **Chill the Mixture**
   Refrigerate for at least 2 hours until well chilled.
3. **Churn the Ice Cream**
   Pour the chilled mixture into an ice cream maker and churn according to the manufacturer's instructions.
4. **Add Red Bean Paste**
   During the last few minutes of churning, add spoonfuls of sweetened red bean paste and gently fold it into the ice cream.
5. **Freeze and Serve**
   Transfer to a container and freeze for 3-4 hours until firm. Enjoy the unique flavor combination!

**Brown Butter Sage Ice Cream**

**Ingredients:**

- 1 cup (250 ml) heavy cream
- 1 cup (250 ml) whole milk
- 3/4 cup (150 g) granulated sugar
- 1/2 cup (115 g) unsalted butter
- 1/4 cup fresh sage leaves
- 1 tsp vanilla extract

**Instructions:**

1. **Brown the Butter**
   In a saucepan, melt the butter over medium heat. Add the sage leaves and cook until the butter is golden brown and has a nutty aroma, about 5-7 minutes. Remove from heat and let cool slightly.
2. **Combine Ingredients**
   In a bowl, whisk together the heavy cream, whole milk, sugar, browned butter (with sage), and vanilla extract until smooth.
3. **Chill the Mixture**
   Refrigerate for at least 2 hours until well chilled.
4. **Churn the Ice Cream**
   Pour the chilled mixture into an ice cream maker and churn according to the manufacturer's instructions.
5. **Freeze and Serve**
   Transfer to a container and freeze for 3-4 hours until firm. Enjoy the rich and savory flavor!

# Beet and Goat Cheese Ice Cream

## Ingredients:

- 1 cup (250 ml) heavy cream
- 1 cup (250 ml) whole milk
- 3/4 cup (150 g) granulated sugar
- 1 cup cooked and pureed beets
- 1/2 cup goat cheese, softened
- 1 tsp vanilla extract
- Pinch of salt

## Instructions:

1. **Combine Ingredients**
   In a bowl, whisk together the heavy cream, whole milk, sugar, beet puree, goat cheese, vanilla extract, and salt until smooth.
2. **Chill the Mixture**
   Refrigerate for at least 2 hours until well chilled.
3. **Churn the Ice Cream**
   Pour the chilled mixture into an ice cream maker and churn according to the manufacturer's instructions.
4. **Freeze and Serve**
   Transfer to a container and freeze for 3-4 hours until firm. Enjoy the unique and creamy flavor!